A Shepherd's Cry

A Shepherd's Cry

To Marybeth,
   You are Truly a blessing to Charlotte
and I. You are a joy in His service
to all. We think you for your friendship
and love. May you truly be blessed
in all you do. Keep trusting in
Him.
            In Christian love
                  Richard Stryker

Richard Stryker

To order additional copies of this book, contact:
Xlibris
1-888-795-4274
www.Xlibris.com
Orders@Xlibris.com
768783

CONTENTS

Preface vii

A Friend's Sorrow...1
A New Life Tonight 2
Awake Oh Spring..3
Awake Oh World 5
Christ Strength Alone 6
Cleans Us 7
Come Follow Me...8
Follow Him..9
From My Heart...10
God Came Near...11
God Does Exist 12
He Hears Your Cry 13
He Is Calling...14
Hear The Cry 16
Help Me Lord 17
His Love...18
His Wonders His Power 19
Holy Worthy And All Praise 20
I Am 21
It Was Me 23
Jesus...24
Lead Me Lord 26
Listen Closely..27
Lord Let Me See Your Love.....................................28
Lord Most High...30

Make Me A Blessing...31

My Creator My Friend 32

My Fortress And My Rock..33

My Hope...35

My Plea To Thee...36

My Prayer...37

My Thanks To You 38

No One Like Him 39

Our Love 40

Show Me Lord 41

Sin for Some...42

Springtime 43

Stand Strong 44

Teach Me Your Will..45

The Best Time Of The Year 46

The Cross Upon Which He Hung 47

The Darkness..49

The Gates Of Heaven...50

Trust In Me...51

Use Me Lord 52

Welcome Back...53

Welcome Home...54

Who Sits On The Throne 55

You Are...56

Author's Biography...57

Preface

God's main purpose in coming to earth in the form of His Son Jesus Christ has always been to draw people unto Himself. He desires more than anything, fellowship and love from those He created. As we all face life's countless trials, I pray His Holy Spirit would use these Poems, that I believe have been inspired by Him alone, to write and to draw you close to His Son's side. And realize nothing life has to offer, is greater than His love and gift of eternal life, to all who seek Him. Again I pray that God would prompt you to read these poems, and through them you would come to know this precious gift of Jesus Christ.

Richard Stryker December /1998

A Friend's Sorrow

When friends are feeling hurt and sorrow
And pain that you can't share,
And no words you offer to them can help
Or remove the hurt they bear.

There is nothing man can do or say
To take that all away,
But to go to God in prayer
He knows our every heartache and pain.

For He knows what He is doing
Though we may not see it now,
We must believe and trust in Him
There is truly no other way.

But to share the hurt and sorrow with God
He'll fill that hurt and sorrow,
With His grace and love beyond compare
Just take it to the Lord in prayer.

3-14-98
By Richard Stryker

A New Life Tonight

Holy Spirit full of life,
Fill me with your love this night.

No matter what I've done before,
I know you've not shut the door.

Your arms extended out to me,
As I kneel and pray to Thee.

Holy Spirit full of life,
Come fill me with a New Life tonight.

2-28-98
Richard Stryker

Awake Oh Spring

The winter's snow has passed
And the green, green grass awakens,
As the flowers show their colors bright
And the trees begin to bud and bloom.

The signs of spring are here at last
As the squirrels dance from tree to tree,
And the birds serenade the dawning of the sun
Yes all the signs of spring are here.

There is yet another sign
Not yet known to all the world,
Of a man that came from heaven
To save the souls of man.

Just as the grass dies hack in winter
Then resurrects again in spring,
This man from heaven, has that power
To rise from death with victory.

He has the power to set us free
From all our sin and shame,
He can resurrect our souls
Just as He does the flowers in spring.

He you know will take our sins
By giving Him our hearts this hour,
Let us live to please Him more
So we can live in peace with Him,
Throughout all eternity.

3-28-98
By Richard Stryker

Awake Oh World

Awake oh world, and hear the voice,
Of the one who loves and cares for you.

Awake oh world, and hear the voice,
Of the one who shed His blood for you.

Awake oh world, and hear the cry,
The cry of the one who died for you.

Awake oh world, and know He lives,
He lives, inside of you.

3-13-98
By Richard Stryker

Christ, Strength Alone

As another day is done, I see all that God has done.
As He has saved me by His Grace,
To make sure that I am safe,
From every foe and beast.

As the enemy tries it's best to overtake Gods power,
To show that he's in charge, with every waking hour.

But God has given faith to me, to stand upon His word
And nothing satan does to me will stand against God's word.
And God knows the love I have for Him
And satan lost again.

So stand in the light and the truth of Christ
And He will bring you through, no matter how
Satan temps you Christ will strengthen you.

Richard Stryker July 19- 2017

Cleans Us

As you cleans us from our sin oh God,
Make us as pure as your river of life.
So we can come before you with pure hearts

As we come to your waters so pure
let us be found worthy, to drink of those waters.
So we will no more thirst, but for you oh God.

Keep us oh God were you want us to be.
So we will forever be where you are,
To live and abide, with. You forever.

By Richard Stryker 3-26-1998

Come Follow Me

Jesus said come follow me,
Come follow me all the way
Leave your worldly things behind,
And follow me all the way
I have a place prepared for you,
Come follow me all the way.
My gates are opened wide for you,
Come follow me all the way.

My streets are lined with gold so bright,
Come follow me all the way
Where I will give eternal life,
Come follow me all the way.

Where you will forever rejoice and sing,
Come follow me all the way.
As we praise and worship our King,
Because we followed Him all the way.
No wants we have nor fears to woe,
We followed Him all the way.
No pain no tears no sorrow there,
We followed Him all the way.

By Richard Stryker 3-26-1998

Follow Him

Come follow me, Come follow me all the way
Though your road be rough, come follow me
And your days full of fear, come follow me
Come follow me all the way
And there may be times of doubt,
Just trust and follow me
look ahead to the sky's so bright
follow me follow me all the way
your troubles will seem so small,
as you follow me follow me every day
I have sent my Son to guide your way
Just follow Him all the way
He gave His life for all our sins, so except Him
And follow Him all the way.
And spend with Him eternity, eternity all the way

Richard Stryker July 18 2017

From My Heart

There is no words to say, dear Lord,
But I thank You for each new day.

You cause the stars to shine by night,
And the sun to rise each day.

The birds to fly and sing there songs,
As they go upon there merry way.

But there's a side not all have heard,
That price you paid so long ago.

You shed your blood, and bore the pain,
To remove our sin and shame.

For all the world to know,
Just how much you love them so.

Willingly you gave up your life,
Oh such a great sacrifice you paid.

Forgive them Father, They know not what they do.
No words more profound in all the world than those.

And there are no words, that I could say,
Except thank you Lord, from my heart today.

2-28-98
Richard Stryker

God Came Near

I see a soul, a soul so *beautiful and fair that struggles through each day*
And does not show despair, because she knows her God is there.

Yes she may have her problems, just as many do, I'm sure
But she knows that God is near to see her safely through.

So many times she has seen deaths door, But returned by Grace and
Grace alone. To find that God has not finished with her yet.

Though so frail in body, her spirit stands so *strong as she trusts in God,*
It's in God alone she trusts. I have never heard her lash out because of

All her trails because she knows that God is near to safely bring her through.
And as her days turn into night she knows her God is near.

To bring her through yet another day to share God's love
With you and you and you.

Richard Stryker 2-26-2017

God Does Exist

I believe oh Lord that you exist, I see from the beauty an around
From the rising of the sun, and the going down of the same

I see you Lord in the fields of grain, and as the summer breeze
Blows by, and as the birds sweetly sing their songs as they
Are perched in the meadow trees near by.

And in the mountains so grand, as the water falls stream down
Off the slopes passing by the trees so tall, Could anyone wonder
Your existence in it all.

In the changing of the Autumn leaves. with their array of many
Colors Only you could paint dear Lord. And in every snow flake
That hits the ground. And in the spring time flowers and in the April
Showers. And in the strength you give us day by day.
Even in those times of trouble, You are there to see us through.
And yes oh Lord we do see, we do see you exist because of
All you do.

Richard Stryker 8-01-2017

He Hears Your Cry

As the savior comes your way, call out to Him in prayer.
He will answer your cry, don't you pass Him by.

He's the savior of the world, He sees all your cares and woe's
Just call on Him today, He may not pass by this way again.

He's your shelter from the storm's, life's troubles are at hand.
For satan's on the move, he knows you first hand.

When Christ Jesus calls out your name, don't you be ashamed.
For when Jesus calls your name, it's to save you from satan's reign.

Just let Jesus cleanse you now, with His everlasting Power.
He will wash away all sin, as you ask Him in this hour.
By His Amazing Grace, you will look upon His face.

As He sets you on the straight and narrow path
He'll guide you all the way, to serve and follow Him
Each and every day, so look to Him don't stray.

Richard Stryker July 19-2017

He Is Calling

Are you hearing His call,
He is calling all that will hear.
He is telling us all,
That the time is so near.

He is going to come,
He'll not say when.
He has been uarning,
Again and again.

The signs of His coming,
You can't help but see.
He has proven again,
To both you and to me.

The floods and tornados,
Volcano's and quakes.
Mass killings of unborn's,
That's no mistake of nature.

He has warned us time and again,
To be prepared, for what may come.
And to heed His last call,
To surrender and give Him your all.

Makes no difference what you've done,
Please listen to His final call.
He'll show you love, grace and mercy to,
But only to those who show they are true.

7-26-98
By Richard Stryker

Hear The Cry

Oh Lord, hear the cry of your people
As we call upon your name,

We long to be where you are, oh Lord
Seeing your radiant and lovely face.

Wanting to be closer now to you, than ever
To lay our crowns at your feet, Oh God,

Come Lord and take us by the hand
Lead us to your land of plenty.

Where we will no more want at all
Other than to be with you, Our Lord of all,

All our sins will be, forever gone
Our pain our fears, and sorrows vanquished.

Forever we will be with you, Our God
Praising and worshiping you endlessly, forever.

3-20-98
By Richard Stryker

Help Me Lord

Help me Lord to take each day,
one day at a time.

The things of this world wm soon be passed,
And a new light of day wm shine.

Help me Lord to take each day, one day at a time
For we know not what tomorrow brings,
So let your light shine through me.

And help me Lord to just trust you,
And set your spirit free in me,
So I can pass it on to others,
who are trying to follow Thee.

Richard Stryker 8-04-2017

His Love

Jesus Christ the Son of God, our savior then and now
Did die for us upon that tree, at a place called Mount Calvary.

Who shed His blood upon that day, to set us all so free.
The pain and tears I'm sure were great, but not as great as He.

If only folks would wake and see, That Jesus loves both you and me.
Oh what a greater world this would be, able to live in a world
Were His grace makes us free.

You and I I'm sure have sinned, sometime now or then. He you know
Can cleans that sin, the very moment you ask Him in. There is no pain
to ask
Forgiveness only shame for those that don't. The time is short this may
be the
Hour, Don't let it slip away.
On bended knee, with heart uplifted, please ask Jesus in today. I am
sure you'll
Not regret it. You'll Love him more and more Hill'

He'll open doors you've never known, and guide you day by day.
His love so strong, you can't go wrong so abide and trust in Him each day.

By Richard Stryker 12-6-1978

His Wonders His Power

You have filled the earth with your beauty bright,
As we marvel in your delight,
the star's in the sky, and a moon lit night
and the sun that shines by day

The flowers that bloom as the birds croon there tune
Of the glories and wonders of God

And His promise so true that He has sent you
The promise of Jesus His Son
who died on that tree, at Mount Calvary.
He gave to us all that promise of life
His life that was given for all

Except God's great gift, He's not just some myth
He suffered and died, He did it for you and for me.
So except Him this hour, for He has the power
To forgive and forgive and forgive

Richard Stryker July 18, 2017

Holy, Worthy, And All Praise

I will call upon the Lord, I will call upon the Lord
I will sing Holy, Holy, Lord, I will sing Holy, Holy Lord
You are worthy, worthy Lord, You are worthy, worthy Lord
You are worthy of all praise, you are worthy of all praise

I will call upon the Lord, and I will sing Holy, Holy Lord
you are worthy of all praise,
I will sing glory to the Lamb, I will sing glory to the Lamb
Who was slain on Calvary's tree for both you and me
I sing glory to the Lamb who died for you and me.
I will reign with Him on high, I will reign with Him on high.

I will praise and glory in, I will praise and glory in, I will
Praise and glory in the name of Jesus Christ.
I will praise and glory in, I will praise and glory in, I will
Praise and glory in the name of Jesus Christ.

Richard Stryker 8/01/2017

I Am

Do you need someone to lean on,
I AM here for you.

I AM your light,
In which to see by.

Though you may not hear Me,
I speak through you.

Though you can't feel Me,
I AM your power and strength.

I AM at work in you, even though
you may not understand My ways.

Only in absolute calm and stillness,
Will you know Me for who I AM.

But as a feeling and a faith,
I AM there, I hear I answer.

And when you need ME, I AM always there,
Even though you may not think I AM.
Though your faith in Me, may be shaken,
My faith in you will never waver.

Because I know you, And because I love *you*,
Even as I died on that cross, It was for you.

I AM O yes, I AM THE ONE,
The Lord of Lords, And the King of all Kings

I AM the beginning and the end,
I AM the Life and the Light,
In the world to come, I AM.

6-7-98
By Richard Stryker

It Was Me

A cross, and spikes and a crown of thorns,
Shed blood and the pain were great.
Two thieves hanging on each side,
And a life so freely given.

Who could do these things?
To spike the hands, the feet,
To pierce the side till blood streamed down.
Who could do these things?

To wear a crown of thorns upon the head,
And continue to shed that blood.
Tell me who could do these things?

To be condemned to die,
Two thieves hanging on each side.
One confessed the other not.

A life was given on that day,
So I could have eternal stay.
Upon that great judgement day.

By Richard Stryker 2-24-98

Jesus

Who left His home in heaven,
To come to earth for sin.

To find His sheep that went astray,
To bring them back to Him.

He went to Calvary on that tree,
To shed His blood for both you and me.

To claim His church, the Bride to come,
To tell the world of sin and pride.

That Jesus Christ alone had died,
For all the world both far and wide.

The time has come, this very hour,
To give Him full reign and power.

To take away your sin this day,
As you ask the Saviour in to stay.

And let Him guide you all the way,
As you serve Him every day.

Time alone is the test of time,
To let others see His light shine.

2-26-98
Richard Stryker

Lead Me Lord

Lead me Lord I pray, Show me what it is,

You have for me each day. Help me to grow in you oh Lord I pray. To learn to love others, the way you love me each day.

To live a life pleasing unto you, to be and set an example,

That would be pleasing to you as well. To do your perfect will.

As you guide me through each day, with not one complaint in mind.

To stand my ground for you oh Lord, no matter what may come my way. To spread Your word throughout this land. I'll ask you then dear Lord, To shleld me Lord from all that's wrong, So I'll not bring shame to your Holy name.

To praise and follow you always, that is my prayer to you. Without compromise or exchange. Help me oh Lord I pray. To love you more and more each day, just as you love me.
By Richard Stryker 2-19-1998

Listen Closely

Hear the voice of the Lord as He calls to you,
Listen closely for that still small voice.
He seeks to do a work in you, as you seek His face.
He will mold and make you, as He has you on His potter's wheel.
Trust Him in every way, He will never let you down.
He is always looking for a vessel, that is willing to say yes Lord.
I am willing Lord, use me as you wish.
I can see the tears in the eyes of the Lord,
As you give Him your all. So just listen for that still small voice,
that is calling out to you. Welcome home my child, He says.
Welcome home my child, and well done.

By Richard Stryker 9-2-2017

Lord Let Me See Your Love

Lord let me be found worthy,
Of that price you paid for me.

Knowing how you gave your life for me,
So that I might be free.

The pain the stripes, the blood you shed,
That was all for me upon that tree.

You hung between two thieves,
Though you did nothing wrong.

The crown of thorns upon your head,
As they beat you till near dead.

As they layed you in the tomb,
And gave you up for dead.

Help me, help us the world to see,
Just how much you loved us all.

But now the world can see,
That satan did not have that victory.

His light still shines for one and all,
So listen for His final call.

Let His light draw you in,
Please, don't let satan win.

3-1-98
By Richard Stryker

Lord Most High

I need you Lord most high, every moment of every day.

In all that I do, or in all that I say, I need you Lord most high.

Temptations come to try to stay, any time I go astray.

But with you near oh Lord most high, I find it drifting far away. I do need you, Lord most high.

In joy or in sorrow, you have blessed each tomorrow.

With your love and your grace, you have erased my mistakes. I need you Lord most high.

Come fill my heart this hour, with your wonder working power. And give me strength to carry on, the work you would have me do. Oh yes oh Lord, I do need you every hour of every day.

By Richard Stryker 7-12 -1998

Make Me A Blessing

Make me a blessing, Lord for Thee,
That to others, they might see,
Your light, that shines through me.

There soon coming King,
And there Saviour to be,
As they look to heaven, to follow Thee.

So that they to, can have that light,
That shines, deep, deep into the night.

3-13-98
By Richard Stryker

My Creator My Friend

When I wake up in the morning,
I see your beauty bright.
And I wonder through the day,
I marvel at each sight.

As I hear the birds sweetly singing,
And see the butterfly's pass by.
That's when I think of my creator,
My Saviour and my Friend.

And when the sky is painted crimson,
By the setting of the Son.
And when the birds cease to sing their songs,
Then I know my day is done.

For this is when I bow in prayer,
Forgetting all the worldly strife.
Then I share with Him on high,
All my love for Him each night.

And as I pray to my Creator,
My Saviour and my Friend.
To give me guidance and the strength,
To do a work for Him.

2-26-98
By Richard Stryker

My Fortress And My Rock

Jesus you are my fortress,
And my strength for each new day.

And Jesus you are my fortress,
My Solid Rock on which I'll stand.

All other ground around me,
Is nothing more than sinking sand.

So I'll stand upon that Solid Rock,
Oh that Solid Rock is, Jesus.
A mighty fortress forever more.

The Cross on which He hung,
On Mount Calvary that day.
Is the Cross that I hold dear to my heart.

So I'll stand upon that Solid Rock,
On that Solid Rock I'll stand.

Jesus is that Solid Rock,
No other ground will stand.

So I'll stand upon that Solid Rock,
Upon that Solid Rock I'll stand.

And Jesus is that Solid Rock,
No other ground will stand.

3-1-98
Richard Stryker

My Hope

I've known the highs that joy can bring,
And the gloom of deep despair.

And in every situation, I know my God was there,
To see me through each joy,
And through my despair as well.

My hope is renewed when all around,
My walls seem to topple down around me.

He shows His Grace, His Mercy to,
To let me know He cares.

He has seen my many imperfections,
I've had many from time to time.

He forgives them all right from the start,
He is always there to lift me up,
To show me He cares and loves me so.

3-10-98
By Richard Stryker

My Plea To Thee

This is my plea to Thee dear Lord,
That I might stretch my hand to Thee.
To have you search my heart today,
To bring me back each time I stray.

I know your ways are always best,
Despite what I might feel.
I know Thy way is always right,
So lead and guide me as I go my every step today.

I need your hand to hold real tight,
To let me know your love and strength.
Is all I need to bring me through,
So let your light shine through me.

So all the world will see,
That you live and dwell within.

3-10-98
By Richard Stryker

My Prayer

I pray my words, that an will hear
As I speak His words so clear
To reach the hearts of those around
To show them what came down.

The Son of man had come to earth
To show His love for an
But as you see upon that tree
He gave His life for you and me.

He paid the price to set us free
The blood the pain there was no shame
The cost was high and then the sigh
Look close and see it was for thee He died
Yes look close and see it was for you and
Me He died.

Richard Stryker July 17 2017

My Thanks To You

I thank you Lord for each new day
And all that it may bring

And as I see the flowers bloom
And hear the birds that sing

I thank my Lord above to know
For all the love He shows and gives
He's done it all for me

I thank you Lord for each new day
And all that it may bring

The lilies white, the beauty bright
I close my eyes to rest each night

And as I wake and see the light
I start my day in prayer with you

And go on about my way.

Richard Stryker July 17 2017

No One Like Him

This man they call Jesus
There is no one like Him,
In this world of sin and shame
There is no other Name, But Jesus.

He can heal your broken heart
Right from the very start,
Just turn your cares to Him
He is there to see you through.

He knows your every need
He cares for one and all,
You can lean on Him each day
He will take care of you.

He can turn your sorrow to joy
Your fears and despair He'll remove,
Your hurt and pain, will no more remain
Just turn them all over to Him.

He has proven His love, time and again
Let us open our eyes, to see His great love,
That great love that is pouring out to man
He has pardon for sin, to all that will come.

3-22-98
By Richard Stryker

Our Love

I have a friendship so divine
That only love can bind
And reaches to our heavenly home
Were God abides alone.

The pain that hides behind her smiles
As I hear her say each day
I thank you Lord for showing me your way.

He draws us close together, as we set and pray
To follow Him yet another day,
As He draws us close to Him to pray.

The lives that see our threads that bind,
Yes binds us close to Thee.
Will see that we so live for Thee
Till we so reach eternity.

Richard Stryker July 18, 2017

Show Me Lord

Mold me and make me and guide me each day
that I can see clearly your path of the way.
Though the day can grow dreary
Your light guides my way.
Just show me your will
In all I might do.
That I will see clearly,
Your path of the way.
So I don't grow weary,
And then go astray
Please Lord just guide me,
Each step of my way.

By Richard Stryker 9-3-2017

Sin for Some

Satan thought his power was great, But Jesus showed him wrong. The gates of hell could not prevail, Against the Son of Man.
No power on earth could ever be as gentle, or as strong as He. There is no match for His great power, to take away those keys. For death will sting, for some I'm sure.
But not for us all, He gives His call, for one and all.

Don't get trapped by satans tricks, He sets them up more and more. For death will sting, for some I'm sure
Unless we heed His gentle call, Our Saviour has for one and all.

7-12-1998

By Richard Stryker

Springtime

We see the flowers blooming
And smell the crisp new air,
As we go about our day
We know that Gods been there.

The birds that sing there melody
As the butterflies pass by,
They seem to know that spring has come
By the promise our God has made.

The rebirth of all around us
Indeed a miracle has come,
Yes it is that promise God has made
It's His resurrection power here on earth,
Of eternal life with each new birth.

3-14-98
By Richard Stryker

Stand Strong

Stand strong in the midst of the storm,
Christ is there. He is calling out to you
Hold on my child, hold on I am here

He sees when you are hearting and in pain
He calls out to you, come to me,
and I will give you rest. And a calm and a peace
that no other can give.

I will wrap my arms of love around you
To shelter you from the storm.
I may not take you out of the storm,
But I will bring you through and be there with you.

I will comfort you in your pain and give you strength
In every situation trust in me, now and always.
I am Christ your King and your salvation.

Richard Stryker July 18-2017

Teach Me Your Will

Lord teach me your will as I go through each day,
Show me and guide me each step of the way.
Help me to listen for your gentle voice,
To teach me your way as I go through the day.
Keep me from falling and causing you shame,
Help me to be true to your matchless Name.
Let your light shine out from me so that
others will know that you live in me,
Let me not cause you the pain you once felt.
But to show others the way to the cross,
I thank you and praise you for all you have done.
For I know Lord, you are truly the one.

7-12-98
By Richard Stryker

The Best Time Of The Year

We see God's beauty all year long as the birds do sing their songs
As the flowers bloom in spring and summer shows its spread
There comes a time in fall known to us all as we see the colors change
To the harvest of the year, we then call it Autumn Time
To me the best time of the year God's best time to show His handy work
As He paints the trees of beauty, with every color of the rainbow bright
So we marvel in His delight and know that He is the creator of it all.

He shows His love for one and all, and calls us to His side
And says to us both far and wide, See I've done this all for thee.
So I ask both one and all just remember me.

Richard Stryker July 18 2017

The Cross Upon Which He Hung

Oh the Cross that stood upon that hill
Was the Cross that saved us all,
I will love and cherish that Old Rugged Cross
Because of what Christ did for me,
All because of Calvary.

The suffering and the shame
All to save a wretch like me,
No words could ever say, what's in my heart today
Because of what Christ did for me,
All because of Calvary.

The blood He shed was so divine
It streamed from Calvary's Hill,
To set us all so free
All because of what Christ did for me,
All because of Calvary.

He gave up His life so freely indeed
To show of His love for both you and me,
No other could do what Christ has done
All because of what Christ did for me,
All because of Calvary.

He died on that Cross
He then rose from the dead,
Just as He said He would
All because of what Christ did for me
All because of Calvary.

He said He would come again
To judge the living and the dead,
So be ready for His coming
All because of what Christ did for me,
All because of Calvary.

3-17-98
By Richard Stryker

The Darkness

Though the darkness of night, is as black as can be,
Sin seems to lurk all around.
But I know in that night so full of black and despair,
A light seems to shine, so clear and so bright,
To cleans us from all sin and despair.
Just call out His name, you'll not be the same
For Christ Jesus is the Light of the world.

By Richard Stryker 9-3-2017

The Gates Of Heaven

The gates of heaven are opened,
Are opened for all who believe.
The words that are written,
Are the words that God has wrote.
Don't doubt them, just obey.

Love so divine, as long as we're on time,
To meet Him on that great judgement day.
Yes the gates of heaven are opened,
Are opened for all who believe.
They're opened for you and for me.

3-6-76
By Richard Stryker

Trust In Me

In the midst of your storm, I'll be there for you
Your trials may be many, you can count on me
I will see you through.
I see your heart and I feel your pain,
But know I am there for you
And I know it's hard to trust in those you love
But know that I am one you can always trust in.
And I Am one that will always love you,
Because you are my child, and I have you covered
With my blood, all I ask is to accept me and trust me
For I am your salvation, and your eternity, and I
Am the light of the world to come.

Richard Stryker July 18, 2017

Use Me Lord

Use me Lord as I awake
To start my day with you
Help me to see what you have in store
As you lead me through my day
This world is hard and cold at times
But with your love in me I know
I can lead others straight to Thee
As you guide me through my day.
With my mouth that I might speak,
The words you would have me to say.
And with my hands you would have me
Help rebuild whatever has been destroyed.
And use my feet to carry me where ever you may lead
That I can do whatever task you have in store for me.
Until I've reached eternity.

By Richard Stryker 8-30-2017

Welcome Back

Give glory and honor and praise to the Lamb
Give glory and honor and praise to Him.

He is seeking that one who has gone astray
To fill your heart with His love today

We know not the hour, But He has the power
To forgive, and forget all your past.
Welcome back my child, welcome back.

By Richard Stryker 9-2-2017

Welcome Home

In this world of life's uncertainty's, things can change in just one moment
Yet it is very clear to see, there is a day and time coming down the road
That all things will become very clear, it will be our final call.
The call from the Lord above, to say. It is that time I have set aside for you
To bring you home to be with me. Where there will be no more tears no pain
And no sorrow here. To lay your crowns at the feet of Jesus, as He welcomes
You home. To a great celebration to dine at the banquet table of the Lamb of Glory.
Where we will dwell and reign with Him on high for all eternity.

By Richard Stryker 8-30-2017

Who Sits On The Throne

Give glory and honor to the great I Am, Give glory and honor to the Lamb that was slain.
Give glory and honor and praise to the King of all King's.
Give glory and honor to Him on the Throne, The judge of all men is He.

Give glory and honor to the great I AM, Give glory and honor to the Lamb that was slain.
Give glory and honor to the King of all King's, Give glory and honor to Him on the throne.
The judge of all men is He. Christ Jesus the King of all King's

Give glory and honor to the one who arose and captured the keys from the grave.
Give glory and honor to the great I AM give glory and honor to the one who sits on the throne.
Give glory and honor to the King of all King's, who was and is and is to come.

By Richard Stryker 8-4-2017

You Are

Come Lord, fill us with your presence
Let us worship, and bow down before you
You are our strength and our power.

You are our mighty shield about us.
We are fed day by day on your word.
We long to see your face Mighty One.

We will forever praise your Holy Name
You are the Rock on which we stand,
There is none like you oh God.

You are the joy in which we delight
You are the sacrifice that has saved us.
You are the Lamb, and the most high God.

Perfect and pure in every way,
There is no other god but you.
You are the breath in which we breathe
You are the King of Kings
You are the Lord of Lords,
You are the beginning and the end.

By Richard Stryker 3-28-98

Author's Biography

 I've worked as an Anesthesia Technician for over 35 years and have since retired. I served in the Army as a Truck Drive and have a profound love for my country. I've been married over 43 years, and I've been a Christian for 42 of those years, and my number one love is for the Lord; He is my Rock on which I stand. For the past 50 years, I've been writing Poems and have been encouraged by several individuals to have my Poems published. I have many to thank for encouraging me to actually write my Poems out.

Printed in the United States
By Bookmasters